Dedicated to

Buddha

Preface

In this book, we embark on a journey to explore the profound teachings of Zen through the art of origami.

Just as paper transforms with each crease, so too does the mind, opening to the wisdom found in simplicity and stillness. Let these folded forms be your guide, revealing the quiet truths that have always been present, waiting to be seen.

CONTENTS

Introduction

Have you ever wondered that a sheet of paper is like life, plain until it is touched?

With every crease it becomes something new, just as our lives are shaped by the moments we live. Moments fold into memories, challenges fold into growth, silence folds into wisdom.

Join us on this creative journey to reflect on life through the mindful art of origami.

Kangaroo

The origami kangaroo embodies the wisdom of intentional living, showing us that true peace comes not from movement alone, but from carrying what truly matters.

Its every fold reflects the harmony between holding on to what nurtures us and releasing what no longer serves us.

It is a lesson in balance, teaching us to embrace life's momentum while nurturing what is precious along the way.

Flow with Purpose

Ride the Present

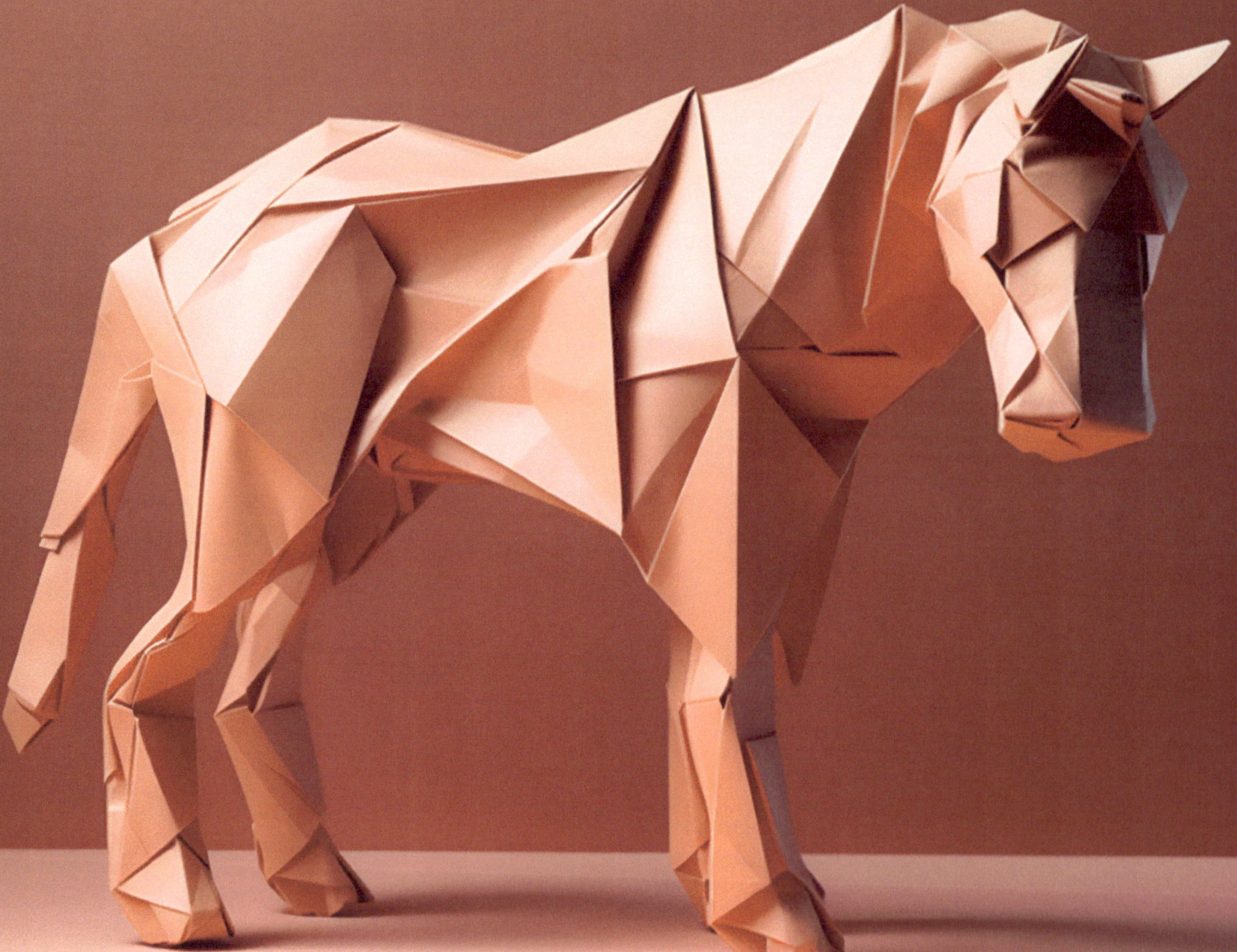

Horse

The horse in origami embodies the philosophy of mindful movement, reminding us that true presence lies not in rushing, but in being fully aware of each step.

Its graceful form reflects the rhythm of intention, where each motion flows with purpose.

Through its elegance, it guides us to ride life's momentum with clarity, embracing each moment with focused awareness.

Dolphin

The dolphin origami captures the essence of playful energy, showing us that true freedom lies not in restraint but in embracing life's natural currents.

It serves as a reminder that presence is not about control but about moving in harmony with the moment.

Through its grace, it guides us to navigate life's waves with joy, embracing each moment with playful awareness and a free spirit.

Embrace the Tide

Walk the Path Within

Stag

The stag in origami embodies the Zen philosophy of honoring instincts, serving as a reminder to trust the wisdom that naturally resides within.

Its poised form embodies quiet strength, moving with certainty rather than resistance.

Through its elegance, it reminds us to move through life with clarity and trust in our inner compass.

Fox

The fox origami embodies the philosophy of adaptability, reminding us that true wisdom lies not in rigidity, but in the flow of change.

Its sleek form reveals that presence is found in movement, adjusting with ease rather than resisting change.

Through its agile shape, it guides us to face life's uncertainties with confidence, embracing challenges with openness.

Sway with the Winds

Crow

In the crow, we find the Zen philosophy of seeing beyond appearances, where true insight emerges from observing what lies beneath the surface.

Its sharp gaze reminds us that wisdom is not in what is obvious, but in the patience to notice what others overlook.

Through its quiet vigilance, it teaches us to find clarity, uncovering depth in the ordinary and truth through perception.

See Beyond the Surface

Rooster

The rooster origami embodies the philosophy of awakening, reminding us that true presence lies not in the past or future, but in the now.

Its bold stance reflects the clarity that presence brings, meeting each moment with steady focus.

With its vibrant energy, it calls us to embrace life's rhythm, welcoming each moment with keen awareness and openness.

Stay Alert

Own Your Story

Rhino

In the form of rhino origami, we find the philosophy of embracing our scars, teaching us that true strength lies in owning every mark that shapes us.

Its robust form speaks of perseverance, showing that resilience is not in avoiding hardship but in carrying it with dignity.

Through its grounded presence, it teaches us to stand tall in who we've become, wearing our journey with pride.

Crane

In the crane, we find the Zen philosophy of wu wei, where effortless action flows in harmony with the natural rhythm of life.

Its graceful movements embody ease, showing that true strength lies in moving with, not against, the flow.

Through its elegance, it teaches us to achieve more by aligning with nature, finding peace in the art of effortless being.

Align with Nature

Giraffe

In the giraffe, we see the Zen philosophy of rising above, where perspective reveals clarity and wisdom beyond immediate circumstances.

Its towering height invites us to see from a higher vantage, discovering insight that only distance can bring.

Through its gentle poise, it teaches us to approach life with calm awareness, finding harmony in seeing the bigger picture.

Elevate Your Perspective

Bear

The bear origami embodies the philosophy of acceptance, reminding us that true contentment lies not in being selective, but in embracing what comes.

Its powerful form teaches that Zen is not about picky choices, but about embracing all paths.

With its grounded strength, it teaches us to move through life without attachment, finding peace in every experience.

Rest in Contentment

Embrace Chaos with Serenity

Capybara

The capybara reflects the philosophy of peaceful coexistence, reminding us that true harmony is found in connection, not in solitude.

Its tranquil nature teaches that peace is not passive, but the balance between stillness and active engagement with the world.

With its calm demeanor, it guides us to navigate life's chaos with serenity, embracing each interaction with quiet acceptance.

Pig

The pig origami embodies the philosophy of humble acceptance, reminding us that true contentment lies not in perfection, but in embracing our authentic selves.

Its rounded form teaches that Zen is not about striving for grandeur, but about finding peace in simplicity & imperfection.

Through its gentle curves, it invites us to live in the present, embracing ourselves as we are, finding wisdom in humility.

Let Humility Guide You

Live Between Extremes

Wolf

The wolf origami embodies the philosophy of balance, reminding us that true harmony lies not in isolation, but in the mindful integration of solitude and togetherness.

Its sleek form teaches that Zen is found not in extremes but in the quiet equilibrium between independence and unity.

With its strength and grace, it guides us to embrace the world, finding balance in both solitude and connection.

Duck

In the duck, we discover the Zen philosophy of embracing duality, where serenity on the surface and effort beneath unite to create perfect balance.

Its gliding grace reveals how stillness and motion coexist, each complementing the other in harmony.

Through this balance, it teaches us to accept life's contrasts, finding peace and wisdom in their unity.

Seek Unity in Differences

OX

The Ox origami embodies the philosophy of steady perseverance, reminding us that true strength lies not in force, but in patient, consistent effort.

Its solid form teaches that Zen is not about avoiding hardship, but about embracing the grind with equanimity and focus.

Through its grounded presence, it teaches that mastery arises from patience, discipline, and quiet determination.

Focus on Steady Effort

Adapt to Evolve

Chameleon

Through the chameleon, we uncover the Zen philosophy of self-awakening, where true enlightenment comes from our ability to evolve and see the world with fresh eyes.

Its shifting colors remind us that wisdom is not rigid but ever-expanding, deepening as we adapt to life's changes.

By embracing transformation, we find clarity in the present moment and freedom in the flow of existence.

Turtle

The turtle origami symbolizes Zen's embrace of slow, steady progress, reminding us that true growth comes from patience, not rush.

Its humble form reminds us that Zen values the journey, finding strength in each small, deliberate step.

With its quiet wisdom, it teaches us that presence, not speed, leads to lasting fulfillment.

Take Deliberate Steps

Dinosaur

The dinosaur embodies the Zen philosophy of impermanence, reminding us that life's essence lies not in permanence, but in embracing change with quiet acceptance.

Its ancient presence reveals that all things evolve, teaching us to move with the natural rhythm of existence.

Through its legacy, it guides us to face life's fleeting moments with grace, honoring change as part of our journey.

Welcome Life's Flow

End-Note

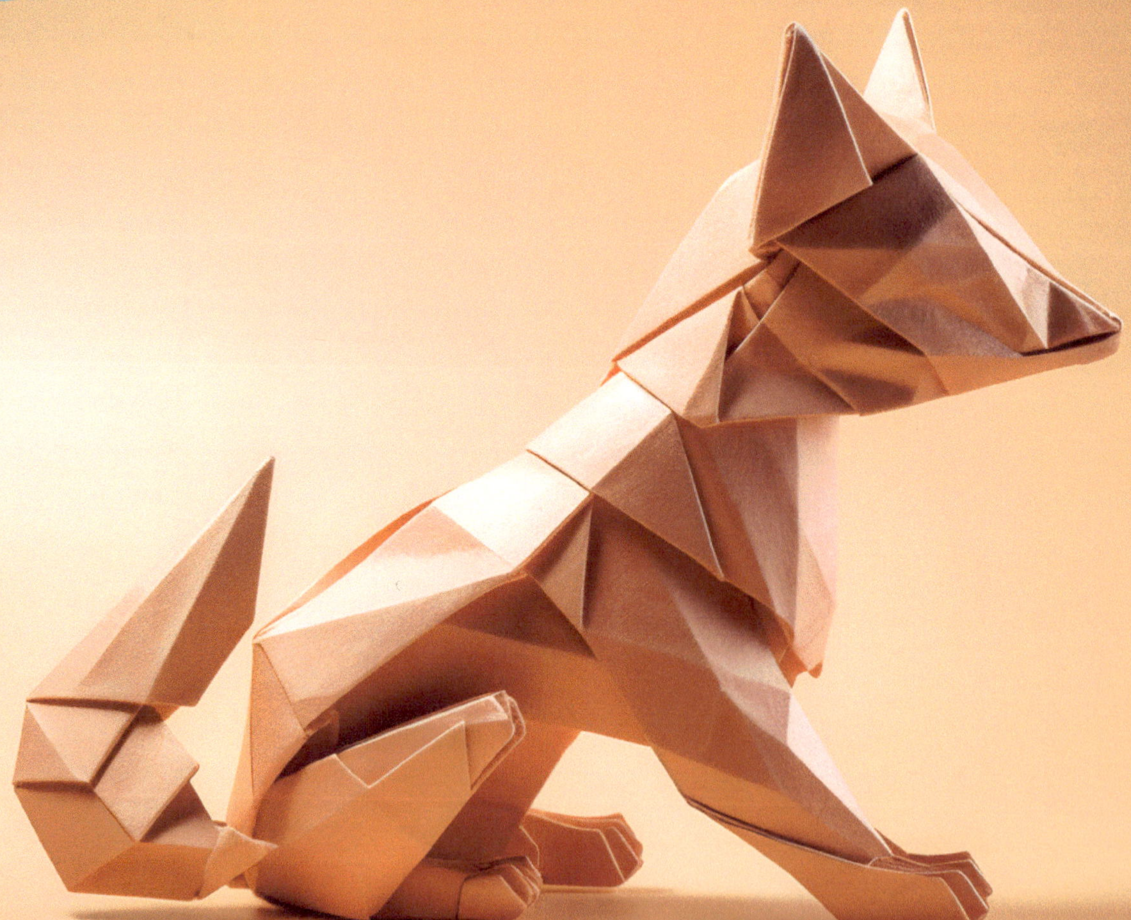

As we fold the final crease and complete our journey through the wisdom of origami animals, we are reminded that the beauty of Zen lies in its simplicity and depth.

Each fold, each shape, and each lesson mirrors the intricacies of life; inviting us to pause, reflect, and embrace the present moment with clarity and purpose.
Let these folded forms inspire you to see the extraordinary within the ordinary.

Review

www.ingramcontent.com/pod-product-compliance
Ingram Content Group UK Ltd.
Pitfield, Milton Keynes, MK11 3LW, UK
UKHW061436190726
13845UKWH00022B/181